Poetry for You

Edward Lear

Edited by Edward Mendelson

Illustrated by Laura Huliska-Beith

SCHOLASTIC INC.

New York Toronto London Auckland Sydney

Mexico City New Delhi Hong Kong Buenos Aires

Again for James
—E.M.

Pencil sketch of Edward Lear by Wilhelm Marstrand on page 4 by courtesy of the National Portrait Gallery, London

ISBN 0-439-39734-0

12 11 10 9 8 7 6 5 4 3 2 1 2 3 4 5 6 7/0

Printed in the U.S.A. 24

First Scholastic printing, March 2002

Contents

INTRODUCTION

Edward Lear was happy when he was talking with children or writing poems and stories for them—but sad when doing almost anything else. He earned his living by making paintings of birds and landscapes that were sold to people who included them in books or hung them on their walls.

Born in London in 1812, Lear spent most of his life away from England. He traveled through Greece, Egypt, and India, making paintings of scenery and animals that were published and praised in his native country. Most of his adult life was spent in Italy, in small houses with gardens that he tended lovingly, and he died in one of those houses in 1888. Lear's landscape and animal paintings were so well-known that Queen Victoria hired him to be her painting teacher, and she was delighted by how well he taught her. But the landscapes and animals he most loved were the ones he created in his imagination so that children could enjoy them.

The places Lear loved had names like the Jellybolee or the Chankly Bore, and the animals had names like the Scroobious Pip and the Quangle Wangle. His poems and songs about them are full of joy and rhythm, and not quite as nonsensical as they sometimes sound, because Lear was intensely interested in justice and freedom. The characters in his poems—both the human ones and the made-up animals—are also passionate seekers of justice and freedom. No matter how ridiculous they sound, they almost always refuse to do what others expect of them. No matter how small and weak, they are brave and adventurous, and many of them find joy in a country far away from the one in which they began.

Edward Lear was the twentieth of his parents' twenty-one children. In such a large family, parents have little attention to give each of their children, and the young Edward probably passed much of his time in his own imaginative world. We know very little about his early years, except that his stockbroker father appears to have gone bankrupt when Edward was four. Edward received most of his education from his sisters and went to school only briefly, starting at age eleven. He never learned to spell correctly, even though he eventually learned to speak Italian, French, and Greek. He seems to have taught himself to draw by copying pictures from books. In his teens, Edward gradually lost touch with most of his family, except for three of his sisters whom he was especially close to, and set out on his own to make his living in London by selling his drawings.

From adolescence onward, Lear suffered from a mild form of the mysterious disease epilepsy, which causes brief unpredictable episodes called seizures, when the sufferer may lose consciousness or make sudden involuntary movements. Lear constantly worried about when his next seizure might occur, and his unhappiness was increased by his mistaken suspicion that the disease was somehow his own fault. He freed himself from this mistake near the end of his life, but too late to undo the emotional harm it had done him earlier.

Throughout his life Lear formed close friendships with men and women, but was unhappy in love. He never married, and only once seems to have found the courage to ask a woman to marry him. She was one of his longtime friends, but she was much younger than he was and refused him. Lear remained friendly with her, but for the rest of his life he thought wistfully about what life would have been like if she had said yes.

Like many lonely people, Lear loved animals of all kinds, both the real ones that he painted and the imaginary ones that he wrote poems about. When he visited India as an old man, he wanted to ride on an elephant and perhaps his wish was granted since he did draw many comic pictures of himself riding on one. But the favorite among all his animals was his independent-minded cat, Foss, who lived to the ripe old age of seventeen. During Foss's later years, Lear called him Old Foss, and wrote about him and drew him so often that he became almost as famous as his owner. After Foss died, Lear lived only three more months.

Perhaps because he received little attention from his parents, who had so many other children to think about, Lear was never especially happy with himself. In the many comic drawings he made of himself, he exaggerated his large bald head, his eyeglasses, and his gigantic bushy beard. He intensely disliked his nose, which he regarded (and drew) as pointy and too large, although no one else seems to have noticed anything wrong with it. Once, in Italy, he overheard a rich Englishman say about him, "Why, he's nothing but a dirty landscape painter." And with a mixture of humor and sadness, he repeated that description over and over again.

Lear liked spending time with the children of his friends and acquaintances, and discovered that he had a great talent for making them laugh with games he invented, and with his drawings and poems. He was once hired to stay at the house of the Earl of Derby to make paintings of all the animals in the earl's private zoo. The earl was soon puzzled to see that his grandchildren were rushing away from the dinner table early. He discovered that they were visiting their funny friend who was eating downstairs with the servants. From then on, Lear ate his meals with the earl's family and the children stayed happily at the dinner table until long after dessert.

The title page of Lear's first collection of poems, *A Book of Nonsense* (published in 1846), gave the author's name as "Derry Down Derry," but it was no secret that Lear was the author, and later editions had his real name on the title page. The book contained poems and drawings that he had written for the Earl of Derby's grandchildren, but the wild humor of the verses and the energetic hilarity of the illustrations made the book popular among both adults and children. Lear's later collections had titles like *More Nonsense* and *Laughable Lyrics.* Lear wanted to call one of his books *Queery Leary Nonsense,* but, perhaps fortunately, he decided against it. In 1886, when a very famous and serious-minded writer on art, John Ruskin, wrote a letter to a magazine with the names of the one hundred works of recent literature that he most enjoyed, *A Book of Nonsense* was the first on his list.

Lear is probably most famous for the hundreds of poems he wrote in the form called the limerick, although it seems to have been given that name only after Lear's death. The form was invented in the early nineteenth century, probably before Lear was born. The nursery rhyme "Hickory Dickory Dock" is an ancestor of the kind of limerick that Lear wrote. It was first written down in the 1740s, and goes like this:

Hickory Dickory Dock
The mouse ran up the clock.
The clock struck one,
The mouse ran down.
Hickory Dickory Dock.

In the early nineteenth century, the last word of the first line of the limerick was almost always repeated in the last word of the last line. Sometimes the whole first line was repeated exactly. The more modern form, in which the last line ends with a different word, seems to have come into common use late in the nineteenth century or early in the twentieth. Though Lear perhaps never saw the modern form, he may have invented it when he wrote some of the poems in this book (they are on pages 43–45).

With their exuberant nonsense and invigorating rhythms, Lear's poems make joyous reading. Part of the fun is making up meanings for Lear's nonsense words—and your guesses are as good as mine. But there is a serious theme hidden beneath the nonsense. In most of Lear's poems, creatures (including human beings) who don't fit into the ordinary world go far away to places with strange names, where they find happiness and their hearts' desire. Each is rewarded for finding the courage to seek his or her own way of life. Standing against these creatures are others who hate anything extraordinary, anything that doesn't obey all the rules. Lear's word for these enemies of happiness is "They." When Lear writes about "They" he is usually writing about people who dislike anyone who is unique, anyone who is an "I" instead of part of "They."

Here is one of Lear's limericks about someone whose physical height was enough to make "Them" despise him:

> There was an old man of Dumblane
> Who greatly resembled a crane;
> But they said—"Is it wrong, since your legs are so long,
> To request you won't stay in Dumblane?"

Here is another of his limericks about someone who merely wanted to dance:

> There was an old person of Slough,
> Who danced at the end of a bough;
> But they said, "If you sneeze, you might damage the trees,
> You imprudent old person of Slough."

Lear's poems are written by someone who always thought of himself as "I" and his readers as "You," not "They." And he wrote them so that "I" and "You" can both laugh together.

The Owl and the Pussy-cat

In the real world birds and cats are bitter enemies, but in Edward Lear's world, a bird and a cat can find happiness in a land far away from the one in which they began. Notice that the Owl and the Pussy-cat take sweet and romantic things like honey and a guitar with them on their journey, but they also do not forget to bring something as unromantic as money.

The Owl and the Pussy-cat went to sea
 In a beautiful pea-green boat,
They took some honey, and plenty of money,
 Wrapped up in a five-pound note.
The Owl looked up to the stars above,
 And sang to a small guitar,
"O lovely Pussy! O Pussy my love,
 What a beautiful Pussy you are,
  You are,
  You are!
 What a beautiful Pussy you are!"

Pussy said to the Owl, "You elegant fowl!
 How charmingly sweet you sing!
O let us be married! Too long we have tarried:
 But what shall we do for a ring?"
They sailed away, for a year and a day,
 To the land where the Bong-tree grows
And there in a wood a Piggy-wig stood
 With a ring at the end of his nose,
  His nose,
  His nose,
 With a ring at the end of his nose.

five-pound note—*a piece of paper money worth five English pounds (at the time, a pound was worth about a hundred dollars or 65 pounds in today's money)*

tarried—*delayed*

"Dear Pig, are you willing to sell for one shilling
Your ring?" Said the Piggy, "I will."
So they took it away, and were married next day
By the Turkey who lives on the hill.
They dined on mince, and slices of quince,
Which they ate with a runcible spoon;
And hand in hand, on the edge of the sand,
They danced by the light of the moon,
The moon,
The moon,
They danced by the light of the moon.

shilling—*a coin worth one-twentieth of a pound*
mince—*chopped meat*
quince—*a fruit*
runcible spoon—*nonsense words that meant nothing when Lear first used them, but in later years came to mean a kind of fork that was curved like a spoon*

The Scroobious Pip

Everyone wants to know what kind of animal a Scroobious Pip might be. The mere existence of something they don't understand makes the other animals worried and disturbed. But the Scroobious Pip doesn't want to be known as a kind or type of thing, and doesn't care about being a member of a category or group. He is simply and only himself.

The Scroobious Pip went out one day
When the grass was green, and the sky was gray.
Then all the Beasts in the world came round
When the Scroobious Pip sat down on the ground.
    The cat and the dog and the kangaroo
    The sheep and the cow and the guineapig too
    The wolf he howled, the horse he neighed
    The little pig squeaked and the donkey brayed
    And when the lion began to roar
    There never was heard such a noise before.
    And every Beast he stood on the tip
    Of his toes to look at the Scroobious Pip.
At last they said to the Fox—"By far,
You're the wisest Beast! You know you are!
Go close to the Scroobious Pip and say,
Tell us all about yourself we pray—
For as yet we can't make out in the least
If you're Fish or Insect, or Bird or Beast."
The Scroobious Pip looked vaguely around
And sang these words with a rumbling sound—
    Chippetty Flip; Flippetty Chip;—
My only name is the Scroobious Pip.

The Scroobious Pip from the top of a tree
Saw the distant Jellybolee,—
And all the Birds in the world came there,
Flying in crowds all through the air.
The vulture and eagle, the cock and the hen
The ostrich the turkey the snipe and the wren
The parrot chattered, the blackbird sung
And the Owl looked wise but held his tongue,
And when the Peacock began to scream
The hullabaloo was quite extreme.
And every Bird he fluttered the tip
Of his wing as he stared at the Scroobious Pip.
At last they said to the Owl—"By far,
You're the wisest Bird—you know you are!
Fly close to the Scroobious Pip and say,
Explain all about yourself we pray—
For as yet we have neither seen nor heard
If you're Fish or Insect, Beast or Bird!"
The Scroobious Pip looked gaily round
And sang these words with a chirpy sound—
Flippetty chip—Chippetty flip—
My only name is the Scroobious Pip.

The Scroobious Pip went into the sea
By the beautiful shore of the Jellybolee—
All the Fish in the world swam round
With a splashing squashy spluttering sound.
The sprat, the herring, the turbot too
The shark, the sole and the mackerel blue,
The flounder sputtered, the porpoise puffed
. . .
And when the Whale began to spout
. . .
And every Fish he shook the tip
Of his tail as he gazed on the Scroobious Pip.
At last they said to the Whale—"By far
You're the biggest Fish—you know you are!
Swim close to the Scroobious Pip and say—
Tell us all about yourself we pray!—
For to know you yourself is our only wish;
Are you Beast or Insect, Bird or Fish?"
The Scroobious Pip looked softly round
And sung these words with a liquid sound—
Pliffity flip, Pliffity flip—
My only name is the Scroobious Pip.

Teapots and Quails

This poem is a nonsense version of an ancient kind of poetry that gives long lists of things, like the immense catalogue of ships that Homer gives in the Greek epic The Iliad *or the catalogue of women whom Odysseus meets in Homer's* Odyssey. *The catalogue in this poem includes just about everything, and even though it doesn't mean much, the poem gets very excited about it.*

Teapots and Quails,
Snuffers and Snails,
Set him a sailing
and see how he sails!

Mitres and Beams,
Thimbles and Creams,
Set him a screaming
and hark! how he screams!

Houses and Kings,
Whiskers and Swings,
Set him a stinging
and see how he stings!

Ribands and Pigs,
Helmets and Figs,
Set him a jigging
and see how he jigs!

Rainbows and Knives,
Muscles and Hives,
Set him a driving
and see how he drives!

Tadpoles and Tops,
Teacups and Mops,
Set him a hopping
and see how he hops!

* * *

Lobsters and Owls,
Scissors and Fowls,
Set him a howling
And hark how he howls!

Eagles and Pears,
Slippers and Bears,
Set him a staring
and see how he stares!

Sofas and Bees,
Camels and Keys
Set him a sneezing
and see how he'll sneeze!

* * *

Watches and Oaks,
Custards and Cloaks,
Set him a poking
and see how he pokes!

* * *

Hurdles and Mumps,
Poodles and Pumps,
Set it a jumping
and see how he jumps!

* * *

Pancakes and Fins,
Roses and Pins,
Set him a grinning
and see how he grins!

snuffers—*metal cups used to put out candles*
mitres—*hats worn by bishops in the Church of England*
ribands—*ribbons*
jigging—*dancing*

THE NUTCRACKERS AND THE SUGAR-TONGS

In this poem, two characters who normally can't go anywhere succeed in running away and finding happiness, even though everyone else thinks they shouldn't.

The Nutcrackers sate by a plate on the table,
  The Sugar-tongs sate by a plate at his side;
And the Nutcrackers said, "Don't you wish we were able
  Along the blue hills and green meadows to ride?
Must we drag on this stupid existence for ever,
  So idle and weary, so full of remorse,—
While everyone else takes his pleasure, and never
  Seems happy unless he is riding a horse?

"Don't you think we could ride without being instructed?
  Without any saddle, or bridle, or spur?
Our legs are so long, and so aptly constructed,
  I'm sure that an accident could not occur.
Let us all of a sudden hop down from the table,
  And hustle downstairs, and each jump on a horse!
Shall we try? Shall we go? Do you think we are able?"
  The Sugar-tongs answered distinctly, "Of course!"

So down the long staircase they hopped in a minute,
  The Sugar-tongs snapped, and the Crackers said, "Crack!"
The stable was open, the horses were in it;
  Each took out a pony, and jumped on his back.
The Cat in a fright scrambled out of the doorway,
  The Mice tumbled out of a bundle of hay,
The brown and white Rats, and the black ones from Norway,
  Screamed out, "They are taking the horses away!"

sate—*sat*

sugar-tongs—*large tweezers used for lifting lumps of sugar out of a sugar bowl*

The whole of the household was filled with amazement,
The Cups and the Saucers danced madly about,
The Plates and the Dishes looked out of the casement,
The Saltcellar stood on his head with a shout,
The Spoons with a clatter looked out of the lattice,
The Mustard-pot climbed up the Gooseberry Pies,
The Soup-ladle peeped through a heap of Veal Patties,
And squeaked with a ladle-like scream of surprise.

The Frying-pan said, "It's an awful delusion!"
The Tea-kettle hissed and grew black in the face;
And they all rushed downstairs in the wildest confusion,
To see the great Nutcracker-Sugar-tong race.
And out of the stable, with screamings and laughter
(Their ponies were cream-coloured, speckled with brown)
The Nutcrackers first, and the Sugar-tongs after,
Rode all round the yard, and then all round the town.

They rose through the street, and they rode by the station,
They galloped away to the beautiful shore;
In silence they rode, and "made no observation,"
Save this: "We will never go back any more!"
And still you might hear, till they rode out of hearing,
The Sugar-tongs snap, and the Crackers say, "Crack!"
Till far in the distance their forms disappearing,
They faded away.—And they never came back!

casement—*window*
delusion—*a false and mistaken belief, usually about something important*

The Duck and the Kangaroo

Many problems threaten to get in the way of the friendship between these two animals, but they triumph over them all, and find enough happiness to take them three times around the world.

Said the Duck to the Kangaroo,
   "Good gracious! how you hop!
Over the fields and the water too,
   As if you never would stop!
My life is a bore in this nasty pond,
And I long to go out in the world beyond!
   I wish I could hop like you!"
   Said the Duck to the Kangaroo.

"Please give me a ride on your back!"
   Said the Duck to the Kangaroo.
"I would sit quite still and say nothing but 'Quack,'
   The whole of the long day through!
And we'd go to the Dee, and the Jelly Bo Lee,
Over the land, and over the sea;—
   Please take me a ride! O do!"
   Said the Duck to the Kangaroo.

Said the Kangaroo to the Duck,
   "This requires some little reflection;
Perhaps on the whole it might bring me luck,
   And there seems but one objection,
Which is, if you'll let me speak so bold,
Your feet are unpleasantly wet and cold,
   And would probably give me the roo-
   Matiz!" said the Kangaroo.

reflection—*thought*
roo-Matiz—*rheumatism (a disease that causes pain in joints like the elbow and knee)*

Z EMMERY
FIDD
3.

Said the Duck, "As I sate on the rocks,
I have thought over that completely,
And I bought four pairs of worsted socks
Which fit my web-feet neatly.
And to keep out the cold I've bought a cloak,
And every day a cigar I'll smoke,
All to follow my own dear true
Love of a Kangaroo!"

Said the Kangaroo, "I'm ready!
All in the moonlight pale;
But to balance me well, dear Duck, sit steady!
And quite at the end of my tail!"
So away they went with a hop and a bound,
And they hopped the whole world three times round;
And who so happy,—O who,
As the Duck and the Kangaroo?

worsted—*a kind of woolen fabric*

The Jumblies

Like many of the strangely named heroes in Lear's poems, the Jumblies pay no attention when told that they can't get where they want to go in the strange boat they choose to travel in. And, like children growing up, when they return from their journey, everyone notices how tall they have become. One stanza has been omitted for reasons of space, but you can read more about the Jumblies in "The Dong with a Luminous Nose."

They went to sea in a Sieve, they did,
In a Sieve they went to sea;
In spite of all their friends could say,
On a winter's morn, on a stormy day,
In a Sieve they went to sea!
And when the Sieve turned round and round,
And everyone cried, "You'll all be drowned!"
They called aloud, "Our Sieve ain't big,
But we don't care a button! We don't care a fig!
In a Sieve we'll go to sea!"
Far and few, far and few,
Are the lands where the Jumblies live;
Their heads are green, and their hands are blue,
And they went to sea in a Sieve.

They sailed away in a Sieve, they did,
In a sieve they sailed so fast,
With only a beautiful pea-green veil
Tied with a riband by way of a sail,
To a small tobacco-pipe mast;
And everyone said, who saw them go,
"O won't they be soon upset, you know!
For the sky is dark, and the voyage is long,
And happen what may, it's extremely wrong
In a Sieve to sail so fast!"
Far and few, far and few,
Are the lands where the Jumblies live;
Their heads are green, and their hands are blue,
And they went to sea in a Sieve.

sieve—*a strainer (water, of course, flows out of it through the mesh at the bottom)*
riband—*ribbon*

The water it soon came in, it did,
  The water it soon came in;
So to keep them dry, they wrapped their feet
In a pinky paper all folded neat,
  And they fastened it down with a pin.
And they passed the night in a crockery-jar,
And each of them said, "How wise we are!
Though the sky be dark, and the voyage be long,
Yet we never can think we were rash or wrong,
  While round in our Sieve we spin!"
    Far and few, far and few,
      Are the lands where the Jumblies live;
    Their heads are green, and their hands are blue,
      And they went to sea in a Sieve.

* * *

They sailed to the Western Sea, they did,
  To a land all covered with trees,
And they bought an Owl, and a useful Cart,
And a pound of Rice, and a Cranberry Tart,
  And a hive of silvery Bees.
And they bought a Pig, and some green Jack-daws,
And a lovely Monkey with lollipop paws,
And forty bottles of Ring-Bo-Ree,
  And no end of Stilton Cheese.
    Far and few, far and few,
      Are the lands where the Jumblies live;
    Their heads are green, and their hands are blue,
      And they went to sea in a Sieve.

Jack-daws—*birds in the crow family*
Ring-Bo-Ree—*a name invented by Lear*
Stilton Cheese—*a strong-tasting English cheese*

And in twenty years they all came back,
In twenty years or more,
And everyone said, "How tall they've grown!
For they've been to the Lakes, and the Torrible Zone,
And the hills of the Chankly Bore";
And they drank their health, and gave them a feast
Of dumplings made of beautiful yeast;
And everyone said, "If we only live,
We too will go to sea in a Sieve,—
To the hills of the Chankly Bore!"
Far and few, far and few,
Are the lands where the Jumblies live;
Their heads are green, and their hands are blue,
And they went to sea in a Sieve.

The Dong with a Luminous Nose

The Dong is one of Lear's few unhappy characters, but despite his sadness, he manages to shine so brightly that everyone sees him even in the dark of night. For the happy ending of the Dong's story, see "The Quangle Wangle's Hat."

When awful darkness and silence reign
Over the great Gromboolian plain,
  Through the long, long wintry nights;—
When the angry breakers roar
As they beat on the rocky shore;—
  When Storm-clouds brood on the towering heights
Of the Hills of the Chankly Bore:—

Then, through the vast and gloomy dark,
There moves what seems a fiery spark,
  A lonely spark with silvery rays
  Piercing the coal-black night,—
  A Meteor strange and bright:—
Hither and thither the vision strays,
  A single lurid light.

luminous—*shining, giving off light*
breakers—*heavy ocean waves*
lurid—*refers to a frighteningly dark red glowing color*

Slowly it wanders,—pauses,—creeps,—
Anon it sparkles,—flashes and leaps;
And ever as onward it gleaming goes
A light on the Bong-tree stems it throws.
And those who watch at that midnight hour
From Hall or Terrace, or lofty Tower,
Cry, as the wild light passes along,—
"The Dong!—the Dong!
The wandering Dong through the forest goes!
The Dong! the Dong!
The Dong with a luminous Nose!"

Long years ago
The Dong was happy and gay,
Till he fell in love with a Jumbly Girl
Who came to those shores one day,
For the Jumblies came in a Sieve, they did,—
Landing at eve near the Zemmery Fidd
Where the Oblong Oysters grow,
And the rocks are smooth and gray.
And all the woods and the valleys rang
With the Chorus they daily and nightly sang,—
"Far and few, far and few,
Are the lands where the Jumblies live;
Their heads are green, and their hands are blue
And they went to sea in a Sieve."

Happily, happily passed those days!
While the cheerful Jumblies staid;
They danced in circlets all night long,
To the plaintive pipe of the lively Dong,
In the moonlight, shine, or shade.
For day and night he was always there
By the side of the Jumbly Girl so fair,
With her sky-blue hands, and her sea-green hair.
Till the morning came of that hateful day
When the Jumblies sailed in their Sieve away,

plaintive—*in a sorrowful, complaining manner*

And the Dong was left on the cruel shore
Gazing—gazing for evermore,—
Ever keeping his weary eyes on
That pea-green sail on the far horizon,—
Singing the Jumbly Chorus still
As he sate all day on the grassy hill,—
"Far and few, far and few,
Are the lands where the Jumblies live;
Their heads are green, and their hands are blue,
And they went to sea in a Sieve."

But when the sun was low in the West,
The Dong arose and said;—
—"What little sense I once possessed
Has quite gone out of my head!"—
And since that day he wanders still
By lake and forest, marsh and hill,
Singing—"O somewhere, in valley or plain
Might I find my Jumbly Girl again!
For ever I'll seek by lake and shore
Till I find my Jumbly Girl once more!"

Playing a pipe with silvery squeaks,
Since then his Jumbly Girl he seeks,
And because by night he could not see,
He gathered the bark of the Twangum Tree
  On the flowery plain that grows.
  And he wove him a wondrous Nose,—
A Nose as strange as a Nose could be!
Of vast proportions and painted red,
And tied with cords to the back of his head.
—In a hollow rounded space it ended
With a luminous Lamp within suspended,
  All fenced about
  With a bandage stout
  To prevent the wind from blowing it out;—
And with holes all round to send the light,
In gleaming rays on the dismal night.

And now each night, and all night long,
Over those plains still roams the Dong;
And above the wail of the Chimp and Snipe
You may hear the squeak of his plaintive pipe
While ever he seeks, but seeks in vain
To meet with his Jumbly Girl again;
Lonely and wild—all night he goes,—
The Dong with a luminous Nose!
And all who watch at the midnight hour,
From Hall or Terrace, or lofty Tower,
Cry, as they trace the Meteor bright,
Moving along through the dreary night,—
  "This is the hour when forth he goes,
  The Dong with a luminous Nose!
  Yonder—over the plain he goes;
    He goes!
    He goes;
  The Dong with a luminous Nose!"

stout—*strong, sturdy*

The Two Old Bachelors

Many of Lear's poems are about people who become happy by doing what they think they should do, not what other people think they should do. But doing what you think you should do isn't always the best way to live—especially when what you think you should do includes cooking someone else and eating him.

Two old Bachelors were living in one house;
One caught a Muffin, the other caught a Mouse.
Said he who caught the Muffin to him who caught the Mouse,—
"This happens just in time! For we've nothing in the house,
Save a tiny slice of lemon and a teaspoonful of honey,
And what to do for dinner—since we haven't any money?
And what can we expect if we haven't any dinner,
But to lose our teeth and eyelashes and keep on growing thinner?"

Said he who caught the Mouse to him who caught the Muffin,—
"We might cook this little Mouse, if we only had some Stuffin'!
If we had but Sage and Onion we could do extremely well,
But how to get that Stuffin' it is difficult to tell"—

Those two old Bachelors ran quickly to the town
And asked for Sage and Onions, as they wandered up and down;
They borrowed two large Onions, but no Sage was to be found
In the Shops, or in the Market, or in all the Gardens round.

But someone said,—"A hill there is, a little to the north,
And to its purpledicular top a narrow way leads forth;—
And there among the rugged rocks abides an ancient Sage,—
An earnest Man, who reads all day a most perplexing page.
Climb up, and seize him by the toes!—all studious as he sits,—
And pull him down,—and chop him into endless little bits!
Then mix him with your Onion (cut up likewise into Scraps)—
When your Stuffin' will be ready—and very good: perhaps."

sage—*a spice (often used together with onion to give flavor to stuffing)*
purpledicular—*a deliberately silly combination of "purple" and "perpendicular"*
precipice—*a cliff*

Those two old Bachelors without loss of time
The nearly purpledicular crags at once began to climb;
And at the top, among the rocks, all seated in a nook,
They saw that Sage, a-reading of a most enormous book.

"You earnest Sage!" aloud they cried, "your book you've read enough in!—
We wish to cut you into bits to mix you into Stuffin'!"—

But that old Sage looked calmly up, and with his awful book,
At those two Bachelors' bald heads a certain aim he took;—
And over Crag and precipice they rolled promiscuous down,—
At once they rolled, and never stopped in lane or field or town,—
And when they reached their house, they found (besides their want of Stuffin')
The Mouse had fled;—and, previously, had eaten up the Muffin.

They left their home in silence by the once convivial door.
And from that hour those Bachelors were never heard of more.

promiscuous—*mixed together in a disorderly way*
convivial—*friendly and festive*

Calico Pie

This is Lear's nonsensical version of the kind of poem that expresses sadness over someone or something that has gone away. The word "calico" at the beginning of each stanza refers to a kind of cotton cloth, often printed with splotches of bright color (a "calico cat" is a cat with patches of color like calico cloth). Except in poems by Lear, calico is not made into pies or jam.

Calico Pie,
The little Birds fly
Down to the calico tree,
Their wings were blue,
And they sang "Tilly-loo!"
Till away they flew,—
And they never came back to me!
They never came back!
They never came back!
They never came back to me!

Calico Jam,
The little Fish swam,
Over the syllabub sea,
He took off his hat,
To the Sole and the Sprat,
And the Willeby-wat,—
But he never came back to me!
He never came back!
He never came back!
He never came back to me!

syllabub—*an English drink made of milk, wine, and sugar*
sole—*a flavorful flat fish*
sprat—*a small fish*

Calico Ban,
The little Mice ran,
To be ready in time for tea,
Flippity flup,
They drank it all up,
And danced in the cup,—
But they never came back to me!
They never came back!
They never came back!
They never came back to me!

Calico Drum,
The Grasshoppers come,
The Butterfly, Beetle, and Bee,
Over the ground,
Around and round,
With a hop and a bound,—
But they never came back to me!
They never came back!
They never came back!
They never came back to me!

The Pobble who has no Toes

The Pobble and his Aunt Jobiska were mistaken in their ideas about how to preserve the Pobble's toes. The Pobble is sad about the outcome, but his Aunt Jobiska manages to be cheerful anyway. You can read the happy ending of the story in "The Quangle Wangle's Hat."

The Pobble who has no toes
  Had once as many as we;
When they said, "Some day you may lose them all;"—
  He replied,—"Fish fiddle de-dee!"
And his Aunt Jobiska made him drink,
Lavender water tinged with pink,
For she said, "The World in general knows
There's nothing so good for a Pobble's toes!"

The Pobble who has no toes,
  Swam across the Bristol Channel;
But before he set out he wrapped his nose,
  In a piece of scarlet flannel.
For his Aunt Jobiska said, "No harm
Can come to his toes if his nose is warm;
And it's perfectly known that a Pobble's toes
Are safe,—provided he minds his nose."

The Pobble swam fast and well
  And when boats or ships came near him
He tinkledy-binkledy-winkled a bell
  So that all the world could hear him.
And all the Sailors and Admirals cried,
When they saw him nearing the further side,—
"He has gone to fish, for his Aunt Jobiska's
Runcible Cat with crimson whiskers!"

runcible cat—*there is no such thing as a runcible cat, because Lear invented the word, and didn't mean anything by it*

But before he touched the shore,
  The shore of the Bristol Channel,
A sea-green Porpoise carried away
  His wrapper of scarlet flannel.
And when he came to observe his feet
Formerly garnished with toes so neat
His face at once became forlorn
On perceiving that all his toes were gone!

And nobody ever knew
  From that dark day to the present,
Whoso had taken the Pobble's toes,
  In a manner so far from pleasant.
Whether the shrimps or crawfish gray,
Or crafty Mermaids stole them away—
Nobody knew; and nobody knows
How the Pobble was robbed of his twice five toes!

The Pobble who has no toes
  Was placed in a friendly Bark,
And they rowed him back and carried him up,
  To his Aunt Jobiska's Park.
And she made him a feast at his earnest wish
Of eggs and buttercups fried with fish;—
And she said,—"It's a fact the whole world knows
That Pobbles are happier without their toes."

garnished—*equipped or decorated*
bark—*a boat*

THE QUANGLE WANGLE'S HAT

The Quangle Wangle gives a warm welcome to everyone, and because he does, everyone is happy. Many of the nonsense words in this poem sound like real words, but there is no such thing as a Fimble Fowl (although there might be such a thing as a nimble fowl), and no such place as the Land of Tute. Crumpets, by the way, are soft English cakes usually eaten with butter.

On the top of the Crumpetty Tree
   The Quangle Wangle sat,
But his face you could not see,
   On account of his Beaver Hat.
For his Hat was a hundred and two feet wide,
With ribbons and bibbons on every side
And bells, and buttons, and loops, and lace,
So that nobody ever could see the face
      Of the Quangle Wangle Quee.

The Quangle Wangle said
   To himself on the Crumpetty Tree,—
"Jam; and jelly; and bread;
   Are the best food for me!
But the longer I live on this Crumpetty Tree
The plainer than ever it seems to me
That very few people come this way
And that life on the whole is far from gay!"
      Said the Quangle Wangle Quee.

But there came to the Crumpetty Tree,
   Mr. and Mrs. Canary;
And they said,—"Did you ever see
   Any spot so charmingly airy?
May we build a nest on your lovely Hat?
Mr. Quangle Wangle, grant us that!
O please let us come and build a nest
Of whatever material suits you best,
      Mr. Quangle Wangle Quee!"

beaver hat—*a hat made of beaver fur*

And besides, to the Crumpetty Tree
Came the Stork, the Duck, and the Owl;
The Snail, and the Bumble-Bee,
The Frog, and the Fimble Fowl;
(The Fimble Fowl, with a Corkscrew leg;)
And all of them said,—"We humbly beg,
We may build our homes on your lovely Hat,—
Mr. Quangle Wangle, grant us that!
Mr. Quangle Wangle Quee!"

And the Golden Grouse came there,
And the Pobble who has no toes,—
And the small Olympian bear,—
And the Dong with a luminous Nose.
And the Blue Baboon, who played the Flute,—
And the Orient Calf from the Land of Tute,—
And the Attery Squash, and the Bisky Bat,—
All came and built on the lovely Hat
Of the Quangle Wangle Quee.

And the Quangle Wangle said
To himself on the Crumpetty Tree,—
"When all these creatures move
What a wonderful noise there'll be!"
And at night by the light of the Mulberry moon
They danced to the Flute of the Blue Baboon,
On the broad green leaves of the Crumpetty Tree,
And all were as happy as happy could be,
With the Quangle Wangle Quee.

grouse—*a large red bird*
Olympian—*refers to Mount Olympus, the legendary home of the gods in ancient Greece*
Orient—*referring to the East*

The Akond of Swat

Lear wrote that the right way to read this poem is to "make an immense emphasis" on the rhyming words in capital letters, "which indeed ought to be shouted out by a chorus." The poem never tells us who the Akond of Swat might be, but there really was a person with that title: he was a religious leader in what is now Pakistan, and Lear read about him while planning a trip to India.

Who, or why, or which, or *what*, Is the Akond of SWAT?
Is he tall or short, or dark or fair?
Does he sit on a stool or a sofa or chair, or SQUAT,
The Akond of Swat?

Is he wise or foolish, young or old?
Does he drink his soup and his coffee cold, or HOT,
The Akond of Swat?

Does he sing or whistle, jabber or talk,
And when riding abroad does he gallop or walk, or TROT,
The Akond of Swat?

Does he wear a turban, a fez, or a hat?
Does he sleep on a mattress, a bed, or a mat, or a COT,
The Akond of Swat?

When he writes a copy in rough-hand size,
Does he cross his T's and finish his I's with a DOT,
The Akond of Swat?

Can he write a letter concisely clear
Without a speck or a smudge or smear or BLOT,
The Akond of Swat?

Do his people like him extremely well?
Or do they, whenever they can, rebel, or PLOT,
At the Akond of Swat?

If he catches them then, either old or young,
Does he have them chopped in pieces or hung, or *shot*,
The Akond of Swat?

Do his people prig in the lanes or park?
Or even at times, when the days are dark, GAROTTE?
O the Akond of Swat!

Does he study the wants of his own dominion?
Or doesn't he care for public opinion a JOT,
The Akond of Swat?

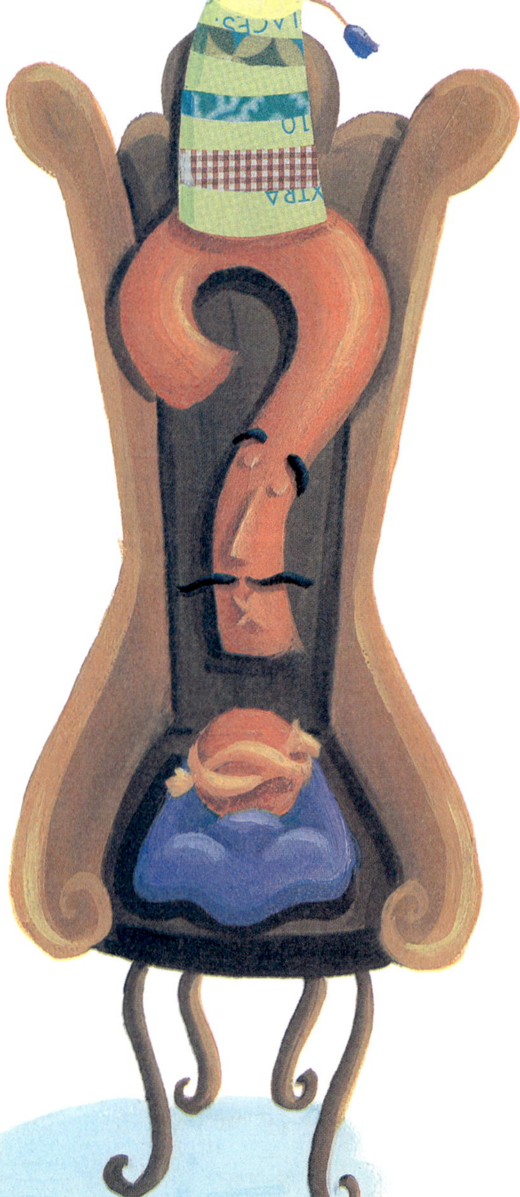

To amuse his mind do his people show him
Pictures, or any one's last new poem, or WHAT,
For the Akond of Swat?

At night if he suddenly screams and wakes,
Do they bring him only a few small cakes, or a LOT,
For the Akond of Swat?

Does he live on turnips, tea, or tripe?
Does he like his shawl to be marked with a stripe, or a DOT,
The Akond of Swat?

Does he like to lie on his back in a boat
Like the lady who lived in that isle remote, SHALOTT,
The Akond of Swat?

Is he quiet, or always making a fuss?
Is his steward a Swiss or a Swede or Russ, or a SCOT,
The Akond of Swat?

Does like to sit by the calm blue wave?
Or to sleep and snore in a dark green cave, or a GROTT,
The Akond of Swat?

Does he drink small beer from a silver jug?
Or a bowl? or a glass? or a cup? or a mug? or a POT,
The Akond of Swat?

Does he beat his wife with a gold-topped pipe,
When she let the gooseberries grow too ripe, or ROT,
The Akond of Swat?

Does he wear a white tie when he dines with friends,
And tie it neat in a bow with ends, or a KNOT,
The Akond of Swat?

Does he like new cream, and hate mince-pies?
When he looks at the sun does he wink his eyes, or NOT,
The Akond of Swat?

Does he teach his subjects to roast and bake?
Does he sail about on an inland lake, in a YACHT,
The Akond of Swat?

Some one, or nobody, knows I wot
Who or which or why or what
Is the Akond of Swat!

prig—*steal*
garotte—*strangle*
Shalott—*the Lady of Shalott was a character who lived alone in a tower in a poem by Tennyson*
grott—*a grotto, or pleasant-looking cave*
small beer—*weak beer*
mince-pies—*pies containing chopped meat*
wot—*know*

Mr. and Mrs. Spikky Sparrow

Like all the characters whom Lear most enjoyed writing about, Mr. and Mrs. Sparrow take very good care of themselves and each other, and they make their children happy in the process. I don't know exactly what you feel when you feel "galloobious," but it sounds very much like the way you feel when you're healthy and lively and free.

On a little piece of wood,
Mr. Spikky Sparrow stood;
Mrs. Sparrow sate close by,
A-making of an insect pie,
For her little children five,
In the nest and all alive,
Singing with a cheerful smile
To amuse them all the while
    Twikky wikky wikky wee
    Wikky bikky twikky tee,
      Spikky bikky bee!

Mrs. Spikky Sparrow said,
"Spikky, Darling! In my head
Many thoughts of trouble come,
Like to flies upon a plum!
All last night, among the trees,
I heard you cough, I heard you sneeze;
And, thought I, it's come to that
Because he does not wear a hat!
    Chippy wippy sikky tee!
    Bikky wikky tikky mee!
      Spikky chippy wee!

"Not that you are growing old,
But the nights are growing cold.
No one stays out all night long
Without a hat: I'm sure it's wrong!"
Mr. Spikky said, "How kind,
Dear! you are, to speak your mind!
All your life I wish you luck!
You are! you are! a lovely duck!
    Witchy witchy witchy wee!
    Twitchy witchy witchy bee!
      Tikky tikky tee!

"I was also sad, and thinking,
When one day I saw you winking,
And I heard you sniffle-snuffle,
And I saw your feathers ruffle;
To myself I sadly said,
She's neuralgia in her head!
That dear head has nothing on it!
Ought she not to wear a bonnet?
    Witchy kitchy kitchy wee?
    Spikky wikky mikky bee?
      Chippy wippy chee?

neuralgia—*a disease that causes pain in the nerves*

"Let us both fly up to town!
There I'll buy you such a gown!
Which, completely in the fashion,
You shall tie a sky-blue sash on.
And a pair of slippers neat,
To fit your darling little feet,
So that you will look and feel
Quite galloobious and genteel!
Jikky wikky bikky see,
Chicky bikky wikky bee,
Twikky witchy wee!"

So they both to London went,
Alighting on the Monument,
Whence they flew down swiftly—pop,
Into Moses' wholesale shop;
There they bought a hat and bonnet,
And a gown with spots upon it,
A satin sash of Cloxam blue,
And a pair of slippers too.
Zikky wikky mikky bee,
Witchy witchy mitchy kee,
Sikky tikky wee.

Then when so completely drest,
Back they flew, and reached their nest.
Their children cried, "O Ma and Pa!
How truly beautiful you are!"
Said they, "We trust that cold or pain
We shall never feel again!
While, perched on tree, or house, or steeple,
We now shall look like other people.
Witchy witchy witchy wee,
Twikky mikky bikky bee,
Zikky sikky tee."

genteel—*elegant, suitable to upper-class society*
the Monument—*a column in London commemorating the Great Fire of 1666*

The New Vestments

Vestments are articles of clothing. Perhaps the Old Man should have known better than to wear edible ones in public, because, as always in Lear's poetry, there are great crowds of angry people who can't bear the sight of someone doing anything unusual.

There lived an Old Man in the Kingdom of Tess,
Who invented a purely original dress;
And when it was perfectly made and complete,
He opened the door, and walked into the street.

By way of a hat, he'd a loaf of Brown Bread,
In the middle of which he inserted his head;—
His Shirt was made up of no end of dead Mice,
The warmth of whose skins was quite fluffy and nice;—
His Drawers were of Rabbit-skins;—so were his Shoes;—
His Stockings were skins,—but it is not known whose;—
His Waistcoat and Trowsers were made of Pork Chops;—
His Buttons were Jujubes, and Chocolate Drops;—
His Coat was all Pancakes with Jam for a border,
And a girdle of Biscuits to keep it in order;
And he wore over all, as a screen from bad weather,
A Cloak of green Cabbage-leaves stitched all together.

He had walked a short way, when he heard a great noise,
Of all sorts of Beasticles, Birdlings, and Boys;—
And from every long street and dark lane in the town
Beasts, Birdles, and Boys in a tumult rushed down.
Two Cows and a half ate his Cabbage-leaf Cloak;—
Four Apes seized his Girdle, which vanished like smoke;—
Three Kids ate up half of his Pancaky Coat,—
And the tails were devour'd by an ancient He-Goat;—

waistcoat—*a jacket worn around the upper body, often sleeveless*
jujubes—*fruit candies that are stiff but not absolutely hard*
tumult—*a loud commotion or disturbance*
girdle—*a cloth band worn around the body like a wide belt*

An army of Dogs in a twinkling tore *up* his
Pork Waistcoat and Trowsers to give to their Puppies;—
And while they were growling, and mumbling the Chops,
Ten Boys prigged the Jujubes and Chocolate Drops.—
He tried to run back to his house, but in vain,
For Scores of fat Pigs came again and again;—
They rushed out of stables and hovels and doors,—
They tore off his stockings, his shoes, and his drawers;—
And now from the housetops with screechings descend,
Striped, spotted, white, black, and gray Cats without end,
They jumped on his shoulders and knocked off his hat,—
When Crows, Ducks, and Hens made a mincemeat of that;—
They speedily flew at his sleeves in a trice,
And utterly tore up his Shirt of dead Mice;—
They swallowed the last of his Shirt with a squall,—
Whereon he ran home with no clothes on at all.

And he said to himself as he bolted the door,
"I will not wear a similar dress any more,
Any more, any more, any more, never more!"

prigged—*stole*
hovel—*a poor or broken-down cabin*
mincemeat—*chopped-up nuts or meat*
squall—*a loud scream (the word also refers to a gust of wind)*

The Uncareful Cow

The uncareful cow is another of Lear's characters who isn't very much bothered by her problems and manages to solve them without much trouble.

The Uncareful Cow, she walked about,
But took no care at all;
And so she bumped her silly head
Against a hard stone wall.
And when the bump began to grow
Into a Horn, they said—
"There goes the Uncareful Cow,—who has
Three Horns upon her head!"

And when the Bumpy Horn grew large,
"Uncareful Cow!"—they said—
"Here, take and hang the Camphor bottle
Upon your bumpy head!—
And with the Camphor rub the bump
Two hundred times a day,!"—
And so she did—till bit by bit
She rubbed the Horn away.

camphor—*a solid oil that used to be given as a medicine*

The Octopods and Reptiles

Octopod is another word for octopus. In this poem the octopods and reptiles know how to enjoy themselves, and even though Lear calls them "a most unpleasant flock," he seems to enjoy their energy and activity.

The Octopods and Reptiles,
They dine at 6 o'clock,
And having dined rush wildly out
Like an electric shock.
They hang about the bannisters
The corridors they block
And gabbling bothering
A most unpleasant flock.
They hang about the bannisters
Upon the stairs they flock
And howly-gabbling all the while
The corridors they block.

DINGLE BANK

Nothing suffers seriously in Lear's world. Even the boys thrown in the sea by their furious schoolmaster swim happily, and some get so much enjoyment from swimming that they turn into trout.

He lived at Dingle Bank—he did;—
He lived at Dingle Bank;
And in his garden was one Quail,
Four tulips, and a Tank:
And from his windows he could see
The otion and the River Dee.

His house stood on a Cliff,—it did,
In aspic it was cool;
And many thousand little boys
Resorted to his school,
Where if of progress they could boast
He gave them heaps of buttered toast.

But he grew rabid-wroth, he did,
If they neglected books,
And dragged them to adjacent Cliffs
With beastly Button Hooks,
And there with fatuous glee he threw
Them down into the otion blue.

And in the sea they swam, they did,—
All playfully about,
And some eventually became
Sponges, or speckled trout;—
But Liverpool doth all bewail
Their fate;—likewise his Garden Quail.

otion—*Lear's strange spelling of ocean*
aspic—*Lear's misspelling of "aspect," meaning location or position*
rabid-wroth—*furiously angry*
adjacent—*nearby, next to*
fatuous—*foolish, silly*

There Was a Young Lady ...

Lear wrote dozens of poems about strange and curious characters. Here are some of them.

There was a Young Lady whose chin,
Resembled the point of a pin;
So she had it made sharp, and purchased a harp,
And played several tunes with her chin.

* * *

There was a Young Lady of Bute,
Who played on a silver-gilt flute;
She played several jigs, to her uncle's white pigs,
That amusing Young Lady of Bute.

* * *

There was a Young Lady whose eyes,
Were unique as to colour and size;
When she opened them wide, people all turned aside,
And started away in surprise.

* * *

There was a Young Lady of Russia,
Who screamed so that no one could hush her;
Her screams were extreme, no one heard such a scream,
As was screamed by that lady of Russia.

* * *

There is a Young Lady, whose nose,
Continually prospers and grows;
When it grew out of sight, she exclaimed in a fright,
"Oh! Farewell to the end of my nose!"

There Was an Old Man ...

There was an Old Man who felt pert
When he wore a pale rose-coloured shirt.
When they said—"Is it pleasant?"—he cried—"Not at present—
It's a *leetle* too short—is my shirt!"

* * *

There was an Old Man who forgot,
That his tea was excessively hot.
When they said, "Let it cool," he answered, "You fool!
I shall pour it back into the pot."

* * *

There was an Old Man who said, "Well!
Will *nobody* answer this bell?
I have pulled day and night, till my hair has grown white,
But nobody answers this bell!"

* * *

There was an Old Man with a beard,
Who said, "It is just as I feared!—
Two Owls and a Hen, four Larks and a Wren,
Have all built their nests in my beard!"

* * *

There was an Old Man in a tree,
Whose whiskers were lovely to see;
But the birds of the air, pluck'd them perfectly bare,
To make themselves nests in that tree.

There was an Old Man in a tree,
Who was horribly bored by a Bee;
When they said, "Does it buzz?" he replied, "Yes, it does!
It's a regular brute of a Bee!"

* * *

There was an Old Man who supposed,
That the street door was partially closed;
But some very large rats, ate his coats and his hats,
While that futile old gentleman dozed.

futile—*unable to produce any result*

* * *

There was an Old Man with a nose,
Who said, "If you choose to suppose,
That my nose is too long, you are certainly wrong!"
That remarkable Man with a nose.

* * *

There was an Old Man, on whose nose,
Most birds of the air could repose;
But they all flew away, at the closing of day,
Which relieved that Old Man and his nose.

repose—*rest*

* * *

There was an Old Man of the Coast,
Who placidly sat on a post;
But when it was cold, he relinquished his hold,
And called for some hot buttered toast.

How Pleasant to Know Mr. Lear!

Edward Lear understood himself perfectly, and although he often wept with unhappiness, he was able to write poems that laughed with joy.

How pleasant to know Mr. Lear!
Who has written such volumes of stuff!
Some think him ill-tempered and queer,
But a few think him pleasant enough.

His mind is concrete and fastidious,
His nose is remarkably big;
His visage is more or less hideous,
His beard it resembles a wig.

He has ears, and two eyes, and ten fingers,
Leastways if you reckon two thumbs;
Long ago he was one of the singers,
But now he is one of the dumbs.

He sits in a beautiful parlour,
With hundreds of books on the wall;
He drinks a great deal of Marsala,
But never gets tipsy at all.

He has many friends, laymen and clerical;
Old Foss is the name of his cat;
His body is perfectly spherical,
He weareth a runcible hat.

queer—*strange*
fastidious—*extremely careful to get things right*
visage—*face*
dumbs—*those who are silent*
Marsala—*a kind of sweet wine*
runcible hat—*runcible is a nonsense word Lear used to describe almost anything, including spoons and cats*

When he walks in a waterproof white,
The children run after him so!
Calling out, "He's come out in his night-
Gown, that crazy old Englishman, oh!"

He weeps by the side of the ocean,
He weeps on the top of the hill;
He purchases pancakes and lotion,
And chocolate shrimps from the mill.

He reads but he cannot speak Spanish,
He cannot abide ginger-beer:
Ere the days of his pilgrimage vanish,
How pleasant to know Mr. Lear!

waterproof white—*a white raincoat*
ginger-beer—*ginger ale*
ere—*before*
pilgrimage—*used poetically to refer to the whole course of a person's life*

INDEX